Ten Tools for Quality

A Practical Guide To Achieve Quality Results

Richard Y. Chang, Ph.D.

American Media Publishing

4900 University Avenue
West Des Moines, Iowa 50266-6769
(800) 262-2557

Ten Tools For Quality

Richard Chang

Copyright © 1994 by Richard Chang Associates, Inc.

American Media Publishing: Art Bauer
                                    Todd McDonald
Project Manager: Leigh Lewis
Designer: Dawn McGarrahan
Cover Design: Jim Beyer

Published by American Media Inc., 4900 University Avenue, West Des Moines, IA 50266-6769
First Edition
Printed in the United States of America

Library of Congress Catalog Card Number 94-70860
Chang, Richard Y.
Ten Tools For Quality

ISBN 1-884926-24-X

Introduction

Continuous Quality Improvement. You've heard about it. You've seen much written about it. You may even be applying the concepts (successfully or not so successfully) right now on the job. The quality revolution is upon us, and unlike some of the other corporate revolutions you may have been through...this one's here to stay!

In today's business environment, things seem to change daily (or hourly, in some cases)! How do you keep up? The answer: Everyone in the organization, from the president to the hourly employee, must be committed to continuously improving all that he or she does in order to achieve quality on the job.

The question that has haunted organizations and individuals attempting to implement quality-improvement plans over the years still rings loud and clear: "What can we do on the job to make quality happen?" Often, responsibility for quality gets pushed up, down, and sideways. From the board room to the shop floor, one can hear the echoing words, "I can't do anything about that!"

Well, you can do something! The tools and techniques presented in this book offer a common sense approach that will help you (a front-line employee, a supervisor, a trainer, or an executive) not only begin, but also sustain any quality-improvement efforts (i.e., process improvement teams, problem-solving teams, self-managed work teams, quality circles, etc.) already in place in your organization.

How to use *Ten Tools for Quality*

This guidebook may be used and referenced during meetings, while working with teams or in your own work area, and anytime you have a question about which "quality tool" to use and/or how to use it.

This guidebook contains step-by-step instructions along with real-life examples. Included are 10 basic, yet popular and effective planning, analysis, and interpretation tools:

- ☑ Check Sheet
- ☑ Cause and Effect Diagram
- ☑ Criteria Rating Form
- ☑ Matrix Diagram
- ☑ Affinity Diagram

- ☑ Process Flow Chart
- ☑ Histogram
- ☑ Run Chart
- ☑ Pareto Chart
- ☑ Control Chart

Continuous Improvement Tools Selection Matrix

When deciding which tool to use for your situation, take a moment to look at the Selection Matrix. Whether you need a tool for planning, analysis, or interpretation, you'll find these tools useful, practical, and easy to adapt for your own purposes.

TOOL \ USE	Planning	Analysis	Interpretation	Team	Individual
Check Sheet		X	X		X
Cause & Effect Diagram		X		X	
Criteria Rating Form	X		X	X	
Matrix Diagram	X			X	X
Affinity Diagram	X	X		X	
Process Flow Chart	X	X		X	X
Histogram		X	X	X	X
Run Chart		X	X		X
Pareto Chart			X		X
Control Chart		X	X		X

Additional Resources

from American Media Incorporated

Other AMI One-Hour Series Books:

The Human Touch Performance Appraisal
More Than a Gut Feeling
Making Meetings Work
I Have to Fire Someone!

Videos Pertaining to the Subject of Quality:

Quality: You Don't Have to Be Sick to Get Better
Good Enough Isn't Good Enough
Good Old Days of Quality Service
Quality Service in the Public Sector

Other Videos Available On These Subjects:

Americans with Disabilities Act • AIDS Awareness • Banking • Business Writing •
Change • Communication • Computer PC Training • Conflict Resolution •
Creative Problem Solving • Cultural Diversity • Customer Service • Empowerment •
Ethics • Family and Medical Leave Act • Healthcare Employee Training •
Healthcare Safety • Icebreaker • Interviewing • Listening Skills • Motivation •
Outplacement • Paradigms • Performance Appraisal • Professional Image • Quality •
Retail • Safety • Sales Training • Sexual Harassment • Stress • Substance Abuse •
Supervision • Teamwork • Telephone Skills • Time Management • And Many More!

To order additional American Media Incorporated resources,
call your Training Consultant at

(800) 262-2557

 AMERICAN MEDIA INCORPORATED™

Check Sheet

Chapter Objectives

In this chapter you will learn to use a Check Sheet as a data-gathering and interpretation tool when:

☑ You want to distinguish between opinion and fact.

☑ You want to gather data about how often a problem is occurring.

☑ You want to gather data about the type of problem occurring.

Steps to follow in developing a Check Sheet:

Step 1: Determine Why, Who, and What You Are Measuring

Step 2: Identify What You Are Measuring

Step 3: Determine the Time or Place Being Measured

Step 4: Collect the Data

Step 5: Total the Data

Step 6: Decide on the Next Steps

The following example shows how a Check Sheet can be used to distinguish between opinion and fact.

Mary had a problem...

...the plant manager had just called her into his office. "Look Mary, we're getting a lot of complaints about damage to the new ceramic mugs we're selling in our catalog. We certainly don't look like a quality company." As manager of the operations unit responsible for the production of the mugs, Mary had to find out what was going on...

Step 1:
Determine Why, Who, and What You Are Measuring

A good place to start when collecting data (whether using a Check Sheet or not) is to go through a process of asking some questions. Questions that should be asked include:

- What is the problem?
- Why should data be collected?
- Who will use this information being collected and what information do they really need to see (i.e., by department, by day, by month, by shift, by machine, etc.)?
- Who will collect the data?

Mary agreed a problem existed...

...(too many customer complaints). After all, the customers wouldn't call and make things up. And besides, the plant manager wanted some answers. Now! Before calling in her staff, she decided to do a little investigating. The first thing she needed to do was to collect data on the situation. Up to this point, the only information she received was from the plant manager. He sounded pretty sure about the complaints. But she wanted facts.

Mary's first stop was to the company's telephone customer service department. There she was able to get a tally of complaints about the mugs from the past two months. She asked the customer service representatives to keep a weekly Check Sheet of complaints about the mugs. Since she wanted to measure various types of complaints over a period of time and get a "snapshot" of the situation, she decided to make a Check Sheet of the complaint data from the previous two months...

Step 2:
Identify What You Are Measuring

Begin by giving your Check Sheet a title. The title should tell readers what they are looking at (i.e., customer complaints for June, service requests for the week of..., reasons for being late to work for the month, etc.).

Next, write only the specific things you are going to measure down the left side of the Check Sheet. For example, if you are measuring customer complaints, possible categories could include late delivery, rude driver, incorrect billing, etc.

Mary spent an hour...

...sifting through two months' worth of data. After reading through it, she decided that the complaints fell into six major categories. She named the Check Sheet "Customer Complaints = +/- 406 Mugs — June" and started filling in her Check Sheet (see Diagram #1.1)...

Customer Complaints = +/— 406 Mugs — June

Complaint Type						
Mug Broken						
Dirty Upon Delivery						
Difficult to Hold						
Mug Chipped						
Poor Ink Quality						
Wrong Color						

Diagram #1.1 — Check Sheet with Complaint Types

Step 3:
Determine the Time or Place Being Measured

Decide whether you want to collect information based on time (i.e., how many things happen per hour or day) or by place, or both (i.e., how many things happen in department A each day, number of defects from machine B per hour, accidents by location or by month, etc.).

Since the mugs have had five production runs...

...Mary set up her sheet with five columns (see Diagram #1.2). She decided to tally the information by production runs, because she thought there might be some trends in the data (i.e., more complaints on certain runs, etc.)...

Customer Complaints = +/— 406 Mugs — June

Complaint Type	Run #1	Run #2	Run #3	Run #4	Run #5	TOTAL
Mug Broken						
Dirty Upon Delivery						
Difficult to Hold						
Mug Chipped						
Poor Ink Quality						
Wrong Color						

Diagram #1.2 — Blank Customer Complaints Check Sheet

Step 4:
Collect the Data

Begin collecting data for the items you are measuring. Record each occurrence directly on the Check Sheet as it happens. Since accuracy is essential when collecting data (after all, you will be making decisions based on this data), don't wait until the end of the day or when you are on a break to record information. You may forget it in the meantime.

Mary entered the information...

...from the two previous months into the Check Sheet. She was surprised by the results. It looked as if most of the complaints dealt with the mugs being delivered broken. At the end of the week, she received the current Check Sheet from Customer Service, and the results were similar (see Diagram #1.3.). She was beginning to think that maybe the plant manager had jumped to conclusions about the production quality of the mugs.

Customer Complaints = +/— 406 Mugs — June

Complaint Type	Run #1	Run #2	Run #3	Run #4	Run #5	TOTAL
Mug Broken	IIII	HHI	IIII	III	HHI	
Dirty Upon Delivery	I		II		I	
Difficult to Hold	III	I	I	II		
Mug Chipped	I	I	II	I	I	
Poor Ink Quality	II		II		II	
Wrong Color	II	III	IIII	II	III	

Diagram #1.3 — Customer Complaints — First Five Production Runs

Step 5:
Total the Data

Total the number of occurrences for each category being measured (i.e., how many times we delivered late this week, how many defects were produced by a machine today, etc.).

After recording all the information on the Check Sheet...

...Mary added up the tally marks for each type of complaint for each production run and wrote them in the appropriate boxes (see Diagram #1.4).

Customer Complaints = +/— 406 Mugs — June

Complaint Type	Run #1	Run #2	Run #3	Run #4	Run #5	TOTAL
Mug Broken	IIII	HHH	IIII	III	HHH	21
Dirty Upon Delivery	I		II		I	4
Difficult to Hold	III	I	I	II		7
Mug Chipped	I	I	II	I	I	6
Poor Ink Quality	II		II		II	6
Wrong Color	II	III	IIII	II	III	14

Diagram #1.4 — Completed Customer Complaints Check Sheet

Step 6:
Decide on the Next Steps

Decide on an appropriate interpretation method.

Make decisions based on fact (not just opinion) about what you are measuring. Since you have data, you can decide how to begin making needed improvements.

Continue to collect data to verify your original findings and to evaluate any changes (improvements) you make.

After reviewing the weekly data...

...on complaints for a month, Mary felt confident that broken mugs accounted for the majority of complaints. Her meeting with the plant manager was scheduled for tomorrow, and she was going to be armed with the Check Sheets for the past four weeks. "Even he," she thought, "couldn't argue with this data."

She also knew if changes were going to be made in packing the mugs for shipment, more information would be needed, so she continued to collect the weekly data on customer complaints.

"Make decisions based on fact (not just opinion)."

Summary

In summary, use the Check Sheet when...

■ You want to distinguish between opinion and fact. (We often think we know which problem is most important. The Check Sheet helps to prove or disprove those opinions.)

■ You want to gather data about how often a problem is occurring. (The main purpose of the Check Sheet is to help tabulate the number of occurrences of a given problem or cause.)

■ You want to gather data about the type of problem that is occurring. (Check Sheets help to break down data into different categories like causes, problems, etc.)

Chapter One Review

List the six steps in the Check Sheet process.

1. _____

2. _____

3. _____

4. _____

5. _____

6. _____

What are the three general situations in which you might use a Check Sheet?

1. _____

2. _____

3. _____

List specific opportunities you have in your organization to use check sheets.

_____

_____

_____

Out of the situations you have listed above, which one represents a pressing issue that needs to be taken care of soon?

_____

_____

Cause and Effect Diagram

Chapter Objectives

In this chapter, you will learn to use the Cause and Effect Diagram to:

- ☑ Categorize many potential causes of a problem or issue in an orderly way.

- ☑ Analyze what is really happening in a process (i.e., the Cause and Effect Diagram provides a picture of the process condition).

- ☑ Teach teams and individuals about current or new processes and procedures (i.e., the Cause and Effect Diagram can be used to train and/or explain how a process works).

Steps to follow in developing a Cause and Effect Diagram:

Step 1: Prepare for the Cause and Effect Session
Step 2: Identify the Effect
Step 3: Identify the Major Cause Categories
Step 4: Brainstorm Potential Causes for the Problem
Step 5: Review Each Major Cause Category
Step 6: Reach an Agreement on Most Probable Cause(s)
Step 7: Wrap Up the Cause and Effect Session

In the next example, a supervisor in the payroll department uses the Cause and Effect Diagram (also known as the Fishbone Diagram) to get to the "root cause" of a problem.

Manuel, a supervisor in the payroll department...

...has had enough! Once again, his monthly budget statement revealed excessive overtime in his department, and once again he was "behind the eight ball" for the variance. "What can I do?" Manuel asked himself. "We don't receive the timecards from supervisors on time, the system is always going down, and the entry process is cumbersome. Manuel knew his manager didn't want any more excuses. She wanted the problems solved, and without excessive overtime...

Step 1:
Prepare for the Cause and Effect Session

Before you begin your Cause and Effect analysis:

- Create a flip chart or an overhead transparency, based on the example in Diagram #2.1.

- Provide a time limit for the session. Generally, 60 minutes is a reasonable amount of time.

- Identify team members to be involved in the process.

- Identify a recorder. His or her job is to write down (on a flip chart or overhead) the potential causes as they are called out.

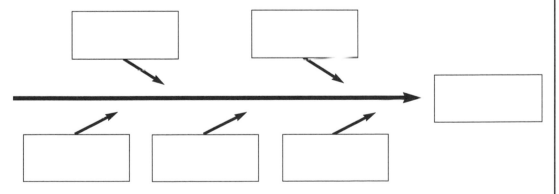

Diagram #2.1 — Cause and Effect Diagram

NOTE: *The recorder does not necessarily decide what category the potential cause belongs in; that is a group decision.*

Manuel decided to call his staff together...

...for a 60-minute meeting to get to the bottom of the problem. He decided to try the Cause and Effect Diagram because he had heard it was a good way to get to the root cause of problems. Prior to the meeting Manuel made a large Cause and Effect Diagram on two pieces of flip chart paper and taped it to the wall of the conference room. He decided for the first meeting he would be the recorder...

Step 2:
Identify the Effect

The effect refers to the issue (problem, process condition) you are trying to change. Write the effect in the box on the right side of the Cause and Effect Diagram.

Manuel began the meeting by...

..."reminding" all those present why they were there: "We're having a problem getting our payroll processed without excessive overtime. Let's put our heads together and try to get to the bottom of this problem." After that he wrote "Excessive Overtime" in the box on the right of the Cause and Effect Diagram (see Diagram #2.2)...

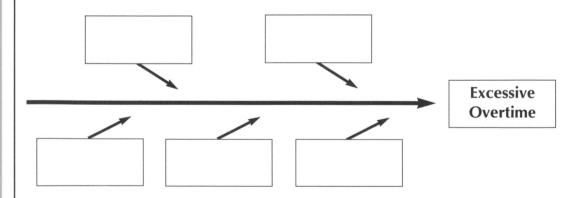

Diagram #2.2 — Cause and Effect Diagram with Problem Identified

Step 3:
Identify the Major Cause Categories

The diagonal lines that "branch" off the main horizontal line of the Cause and Effect Diagram are called "major cause categories." Major cause categories are used to organize the causes in a way that makes the most sense for your specific situation.

Major causes may be summarized under categories such as:

- **Methods, Machines, Materials, People** (the 3 Ms and a P)

- **Place, Procedure, People, Policies** (the 4 Ps)

- **Surroundings, Suppliers, Systems, Skills** (the 4 Ss)

Remember, these categories are only suggestions; you may use any category that helps you organize your ideas.

Manuel wrote the 4 Ps...

...at the end of each of the diagonal lines. The group decided that another major cause was needed. So Manuel added a major cause category labeled "System" (see Diagram #2.3)...

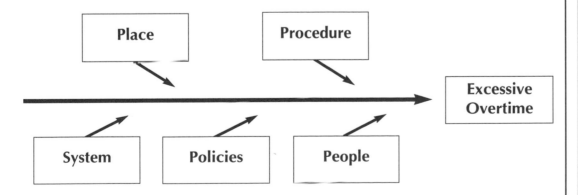

Diagram #2.3 — Cause and Effect Diagram with Cause Categories

Step 4:
Brainstorm Potential Causes for the Problem

Follow ground rules for Brainstorming listed below:

- Don't edit what is said and remember not to criticize ideas.
- Go for quantity of ideas at this point; narrow down the list later.
- Encourage wild or exaggerated ideas (creativity is the key).
- Build on the ideas of others (i.e., one member might say something that "sparks" another member's idea).

As possible causes are called out, decide as a group where to place them on the Cause and Effect Diagram (i.e., decide under which major cause category they should be placed).

It's acceptable to list a possible cause under more than one major cause category (i.e., receiving late data could go under both People and System).

Try to list many possible causes on the Cause and Effect Diagram at this point.

Manuel had led Brainstorming sessions before...

...so he was familiar with the process. As the group called out possible causes, he asked what cause category to list it under (see Diagram #2.4). Some causes were easy, while others were more difficult to "pigeonhole" and ended up in two or more categories. The process continued for 25 minutes...

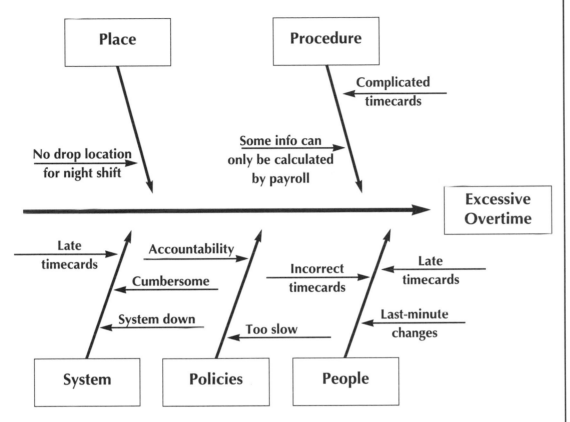

Diagram #2.4 — Cause and Effect Diagram with Potential Causes

Step 5:
Review Each Major Cause Category

■ At this point, look for causes that appear in more than one category. This is an indication of a "most likely cause." Circle "most likely causes" on the diagram (see Diagram #2.5).

■ Review the causes that you've determined to be "most likely" and ask, "Why is this a cause?" Asking the "why?" question will help you get to the "root cause" of the problem.

■ Record the answers to your "why?" questions on a separate sheet of flip chart paper.

When the group realized...

...that a few of the causes appeared repeatedly (i.e., late timecards, incorrect timecards, and system down, see Diagram 2.5), Manuel began asking a series of "why?" questions (i.e., Why do we have late timecards? Why do we have incorrect timecards? Why is the system down?, etc.). Manuel then asked "why" to the answers of the first questions. In doing this, the group sifted through the "symptoms" to get to the "root cause(s)" of the problem. The group felt a little uncomfortable with this process at first (it felt a bit like an interrogation), but soon realized they were actually getting to the "root cause(s)" (see Diagram #2.6)...

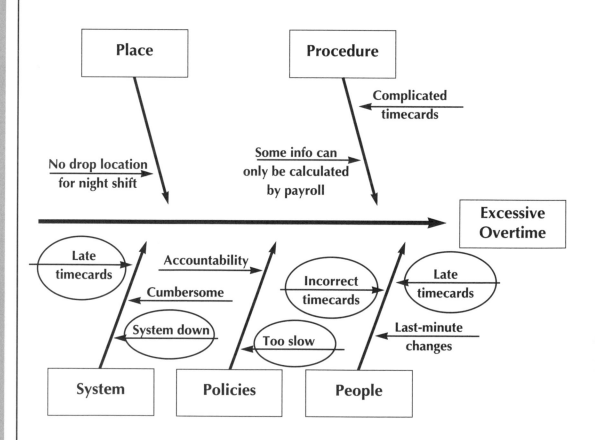

Diagram #2.5 — Focus on Root Causes

Step 6:
Reach an Agreement on Most Probable Cause(s)

■ After you narrow down the "most likely causes," choose from that group those you feel are the "most probable causes."

MOST PROBABLE CAUSES

Late Timecards   Incorrect Timecards

No Accountability   Employees Don't Understand

Lack of Coordination   Complicated

Time Demands on Fridays   No Instructions

Diagram #2.6 — Top Two Causes

After about 50 minutes...

...the group had identified what they thought were the top two most probable causes to the overtime problem. The next step was to develop some type of measurement to determine if they were right. Amy volunteered to find out how system downtime affected their ability to finish keying timecards on time. While Lorna took on the task of finding out where procedures could be changed, Manuel thanked all present for their time and effort and asked the team to meet at the same time the following week.

Step 7:
Wrap Up the Cause and Effect Session

You know it's time to end the Cause and Effect session when:

- The "most probable cause(s)" have been identified.
- Assignments have been made to gather data to prove or disprove the "most probable cause(s)."
- You have thanked the participants.

Summary

In summary, use the Cause and Effect Diagram when:

- You want to categorize many potential causes of a problem or issue in an easy-to-understand, orderly way. (By breaking a process down into a number of process-related categories, i.e., people, materials, machinery, procedures, policy, environment, etc., the team is able to better identify the possible causes of a problem.)

- You want to analyze what is really happening in a process (i.e., by breaking a process down into a number of process-related categories, i.e., people, materials, machinery, procedures, policy, environment, etc. The Cause and Effect Diagram can provide a picture of the actual process condition).

- You are teaching teams and individuals about new processes and procedures (i.e., the Cause and Effect Diagram can be used to train and/or explain how a process works).

Chapter Two Review

1. The _____ refers to the issue (problem, process condition) you are trying to change.

2. The diagonal lines that "branch" off the main horizontal line represent major _____ categories.

3. What method can you use to develop a list of possible causes?

   _____

4. List the specific opportunities you have in your organization to use the Cause and Effect Diagram.

   _____

   _____

   _____

5. Identify and show which major cause categories might be appropriate for your situation.

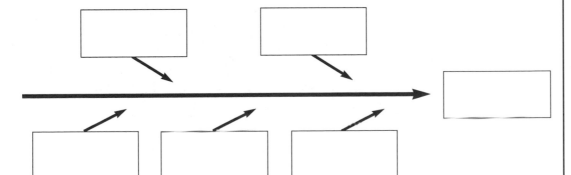

Criteria Rating Form

Chapter Objectives

In this chapter, you will learn to use the Criteria Rating Form when:

☑ You have to select between several alternatives.

☑ You want to make a decision objectively.

☑ You want the group to agree on a decision.

Steps to follow in developing a Criteria Rating Form:

Step 1: Start the Session and List the Alternatives or Options Available

Step 2: Brainstorm Decision Criteria

Step 3: Determine the Relative Importance of Each Criterion

Step 4: Establish a Rating Scale and Rate the Alternatives

Step 5: Calculate the Final Score

Step 6: Select the Best Alternative

Step 7: Wrap Up the Criteria Rating Session

In the following example, a team is having trouble making a decision about which copier to buy.

Ellen, the leader of a team...

...chosen to recommend a new copier for the office, was feeling extreme pressure. Her boss was pushing for the X-Star model, but *Consumer Reports* recommended Quantum's new product; and to top that, most team members favored the Duplicator 4. It was already Wednesday morning and Ellen had to have the group's recommendations to the vice president of administration by Friday at 1:00 p.m....

Step 1:
Start the Session and List the Alternatives or Options Available

At the start of your Criteria Rating session:

- Provide a time limit for the session. Generally, 45-60 minutes is sufficient.

- Have a Criteria Rating Form prepared on a flip chart or an overhead transparency (see Diagram #3.1).

- List alternatives or options available along the top of the Criteria Rating Form.

Note: *You may have to generate these options or alternatives by Brainstorming.*

First thing Wednesday afternoon...

...Ellen called the group members into a conference room. All of them knew they had to come to an agreement on the copier choice issue. Ellen suggested they use the Criteria Rating process to help...

Criteria Rating Form

Criteria	Weight	Alternatives		
		X-Star	Quantum	Duplicator 4
Total				
Summary				

Diagram #3.1 — The Criteria Rating Form

Step 2:
Brainstorm Decision Criteria

You will be judging your alternatives against what you feel are the most important qualities each alternative should have. These qualities are called decision criteria. We use decision criteria all the time. For example, when we are choosing a house to buy, we look at criteria such as cost, location, builder, view, land, etc. If more than one person is making the decision, it's advantageous to agree on the decision criteria. Then the decision-making process runs more smoothly.

Common criteria include:

- Ease of implementation
- Lowest cost
- Ability to meet customer requirements
- Resource availability
- Lowest risk
- Fastest to implement
- Long-term workability

Remember, the criteria may change for each project you're working on.

Ellen turned on the overhead projector...

...which displayed a list she had prepared with a few of the selection criteria the group had "brainstormed" last week (see Diagram #3.2). The criteria included must be able to collate, feed, reduce, and enlarge; must be high-speed; and it must be dependable...

Criteria	Weight	Alternatives		
		X-Star	**Quantum**	**Duplicator 4**
Collate	15%			
Reduce	15%			
Enlarge	15%			
High-speed	20%			
Dependable	35%			
Total	100%			
Summary				

Diagram #3.2 — The Criteria Rating Form

Step 3:
Determine the Relative Importance of Each Criterion

- Give each of the criterion a weight (which represents its relative importance).

- To determine the weight of each criterion, ask the question, "How important is each of the criterion in relationship to the other?"

- Remember, the total of the assigned weights for all criteria must equal 100%.

- The effectiveness of the Criteria Rating process is heavily dependent upon the weighing of the criteria. For this reason the weighing decision must be made by a team with input from all members. This unbiased input can be achieved by asking each team member to weigh the criteria individually. The final weight is determined by averaging the individual weights assigned by each team member.

"How important is each of the criterion in relationship to the other?"

Ellen asked the team to review the criteria...

...and decide how important each one was in relation to the others. She asked the team to assign each criterion a percentage that represents its priority (i.e., 10% would be a low priority and 70% would equal a high priority), reminding everyone that the total of all the ratings must equal 100%. Ellen gave the team five minutes to rate the list of criteria (see Diagram #3.2).

Criteria	Weight	Alternatives		
		X-Star	Quantum	Duplicator 4
Collate	15%			
Reduce	15%			
Enlarge	15%			
High-speed	20%			
Dependable	35%			
Total	100%			
Summary				

Diagram #3.2 — The Criteria Rating Form

Step 4:
Establish a Rating Scale and Rate the Alternatives

"A consistent rating scale must be used."

A consistent rating scale must be used in order to compare the various ideas or alternatives against each criterion. Any scale will work as long as the same scale is used for all alternatives and criteria. An easy scale to use is 1 - 10, with 10 being high and 1 being low.

Each idea or alternative should be "rated" against each criterion using the established rating scale. It is possible that the rating can only be determined after an investigation (i.e., you may have to verify which alternative has the lowest cost).

After the team agreed...

...on the weights for the criteria, they began the process of "rating" each of the alternatives against each criterion (see Diagram #3.3). The Duplicator 4 rated the highest in dependability, while Quantum was rated higher in speed.

Rating Scale: 10 = high, 1 = low

Criteria	Weight	Alternatives		
		X-Star	Quantum	Duplicator 4
Collate	15%	5	5	5
Reduce	15%	3	8	8
Enlarge	15%	7	6	7
High-speed	20%	6	8	4
Dependable	35%	4	6	7
Total	100%			
Summary				

Diagram #3.3 — The Criteria Rating Form with Weights and Ratings

Step 5:
Calculate the Final Score

■ Multiply the weight (established in Step 3) by the rating for each alternative (established in Step 4).

■ Write this figure in parentheses in the appropriate box on the Criteria Rating Form.

■ Add the numbers in parenthesis for each alternative, and write the total in the appropriate box.

■ Write any summary comments in the appropriate box.

After a heated (but friendly) discussion...

...the group agreed on the ratings for each alternative and each criterion. Ellen recorded each of the ratings directly on the Criteria Rating flip chart and asked Patrick, the team math whiz (he was the only team member with a calculator), to multiply each of the ratings by the weight. As Patrick finished multiplying, Ellen recorded the answers (in parentheses) on the flip chart. Patrick then added each of the numbers in parentheses, and Ellen wrote the final totals in the appropriate box on the bottom of the flip chart (see Diagram #3.4)...

Criteria	Weight	Alternatives		
		X-Star	Quantum	Duplicator 4
Collate	15%	5 x .15 = (.75)	5 x .15 = (.75)	5 x .15 = (.75)
Reduce	15%	3 x .15 = (.45)	8 x .15 = (1.2)	8 x .15 = (1.2)
Enlarge	15%	7 x .15 = (1.05)	6 x .15 = (.90)	7 x .15 = (1.05)
High-speed	20%	6 x .2 = (1.2)	8 x .2 = (1.6)	4 x .2 = (.8)
Dependable	35%	4 x .35 = (1.4)	6 x .35 = (2.1)	7 x .35 = (2.45)
Total	100%	4.85	6.55	6.25
Summary				

Diagram #3.4 — The Criteria Rating Form with Totals

Step 6:
Select the Best Alternative

- Select the alternative that has the highest total "score."

- This alternative may or may not be the one ultimately chosen. The alternative with the highest score should be the best. If the team members don't agree, they should review the weighing of the criteria and the ratings and make necessary changes.

  Note: *The summary boxes are used to record any notes about the alternatives.*

- If necessary, repeat the process.

Based on the weighing of the criteria...

...and the rating of each of the alternatives, the Quantum had the highest total (see Diagram #3.5). The Duplicator 4 and the X-Star finished second and third respectively. It was clear the Quantum had won because it was rated the highest in speed, and because it wasn't far behind the Duplicator 4 in dependability.

Although not everyone originally agreed on the Quantum, it was hard to argue with its superiority now. After all, everyone had an equal voice in the weighing and the rating process. The team had reached a true consensus!

Criteria	Weight	Alternatives		
		X-Star	Quantum	Duplicator 4
Collate	15%	5 x .15 = (.75)	5 x .15 = (.75)	5 x .15 = (.75)
Reduce	15%	3 x .15 = (.45)	8 x .15 = (1.2)	8 x .15 = (1.2)
Enlarge	15%	7 x .15 = (1.05)	6 x .15 = (.90)	7 x .15 = (1.05)
High-speed	20%	6 x .2 = (1.2)	8 x .2 = (1.6)	4 x .2 = (.8)
Dependable	35%	4 x .35 = (1.4)	6 x .35 = (2.1)	7 x .35 = (2.45)
Total	100%	4.85	6.55	6.25
Summary				

Diagram #3.5 — Select the Best Alternative

Step 7:
Wrap Up the Criteria Rating Session

You know it's time to stop the Criteria Rating session when:

- The group has come to an agreement on the "best" alternative.
- Assignments have been made (if necessary) to investigate possible rating scores (see Step 4).
- Assignments have been made to communicate the final decision.
- You have thanked the participants.

Since the dependability issue was so important...

...the team decided to further investigate the dependability of the Quantum with other companies who had purchased that model. Denise volunteered to call Quantum to get a list of names. She committed to calling the companies and would have an answer by the following day. Ellen and the team were happy with the results of the session.

Summary

In summary, use the Criteria Rating Form when:

- You have to select between several alternatives. (The Criteria Rating method will help the decision-making process by providing a step-by-step procedure).

- You want to include more objectivity into a decision-making process. (The Criteria Rating method takes subjectivity out of the decision-making process by assigning weights and rankings to each potential solution.)

- You want a consensus-building tool that will help the team reach a decision. (The Criteria Rating method helps to build consensus by taking the "opinion" out of the decision-making process.)

Chapter Three Review

When using the Criteria Rating Form, you judge alternatives against what you feel are the most important qualities each alternative should have. These qualities are called _____.

The total of the assigned weights for all decision criteria must equal 100%.

True or False?

A **consistent** rating scale must be used in order to compare the various ideas or alternatives against each criterion.

True or False?

Decision criteria should be determined by the group through _____

_____.

List the specific opportunities you have in your organization to use the Criteria Rating Form.

_____

_____

_____

_____

_____

List the decision criteria you might use in an upcoming situation. What weights would you assign?

_____ _____%

_____ _____%

_____ _____%

_____ _____%

_____ _____%

How might your choice or weighing of criteria differ if you were working on a short-term instead of a long-term issue or problem?

_____

_____

_____

_____

_____

_____

The alternative with the highest score is always right.

True or False?

Matrix Diagram

Chapter Objectives

In this chapter, you will learn to use the Matrix Diagram to:

☑ Match tasks with the individuals, departments, or functions completing them.

☑ Show a relationship between a task and the responsible person, department, or function.

☑ Rate the strength of that relationship.

☑ Assign accountability and plan actions.

Steps to follow when using a Matrix Diagram:

Step 1: Prepare for the Matrix Diagram Session
Step 2: Agree on Tasks
Step 3: Determine Responsibilities
Step 4: Rate Each Intersection
Step 5: Wrap Up the Matrix Diagram Session

Katherine was president of the social committee...

...and it was time to begin planning for the annual company picnic. She was responsible for the picnic this year and assembled a team of five people from different areas of the company to work on this project...

Step 1:
Prepare for the Matrix Diagram Session

At the start of your Matrix Diagram session:

- Create a flip chart or an overhead transparency of a Matrix Diagram (see The L-Shaped Matrix Diagram).

- Provide a time limit for the session. Generally, 45-60 minutes is sufficient.

- Identify a recorder. The job of the recorder is to write down (on a flip chart or overhead transparency) tasks, responsible individuals and/or departments, and the strength of the relationship.

Katherine called a meeting to clarify the team's mission...

...and to decide how to tackle the project at hand. She knew there were a lot of tasks to accomplish so she suggested using the Matrix Diagram. She explained that the Matrix Diagram would help the team identify the tasks and responsibilities needed to plan the picnic. Katherine drew the matrix on a flip chart and asked Raul to be the recorder...

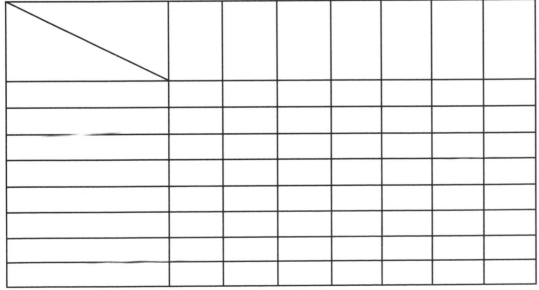

The L-Shaped Matrix Diagram

Step 2:
Agree on Tasks

■ Write the tasks or responsibilities that need to be completed on the left side of the Matrix Diagram. In a group, identify the tasks that can be accomplished by Brainstorming.

Katherine asked the group to Brainstorm a list of tasks...

...that needed to be completed prior to the picnic. The group decided on eight major tasks: food, games, music, communications, prizes, decorations, pictures, and dunk tanks. Raul recorded all the responses on the left side of the Matrix Diagram (see Diagram 4.1)...

RESPONSIBILITY ⟍ TASK							
Food							
Games							
Music							
Communications							
Prizes							
Decorations							
Pictures							
Dunk Tanks							

Diagram #4.1 — Record the Tasks

Note: *The tasks/responsibilities do not have to be in sequential order.*

Step 3:
Determine Responsibilities

Along the top of the Matrix Diagram, list the various individuals, departments, and/or suppliers that will complete the listed tasks or responsibilities.

After agreeing on the tasks...

...the team started to fill out the top of the Matrix Diagram with names of team members and the departments and suppliers that would be involved in the picnic. Each team member was listed, as was the Human Resources Department and a local caterer. Once again, Raul filled out the information on the Matrix Diagram (see Diagram #4.2)...

RESPONSIBILITY / TASK	Katherine	Raul	Roxanne	Maria	Ly	H.R.	Caterer
Food							
Games							
Music							
Communications							
Prizes							
Decorations							
Pictures							
Dunk Tanks							

Diagram #4.2 — Record the Responsibilities

Step 4:
Rate Each Intersection

For each intersection of a task and an individual, department, or supplier, assign a "strength" rating using the following symbols:

P = Primary Responsibility (i.e., this person/group is responsible for the task)

S = Secondary Responsibility (i.e., this person/group helps complete the task)

C = Communications/Needs to Know (i.e., this person/group only needs to be in the communication loop)

+ = More Emphasis (i.e., this person/group has more responsibility than other similar strength ratings)

Blank = No Responsibility

"Each task must have one (and only one) rating of *Primary Responsibility*."

Remember, each task must have one (and only one) rating of "Primary Responsibility," since this indicates ownership of the task. The "More Emphasis" rating is used to indicate a difference between two similar "strength" ratings (i.e., if more than one person has two secondary responsibilities for a task, one might be labeled with a "+" for more emphasis).

Katherine directed the attention of the team members...

...to the Matrix Diagram on the flip chart. She told them the next step was to assign a strength rating for each intersection of task and individual/department/supplier responsibility. A 'P' would be assigned to represent a primary responsibility; an 'S' if it was to be a secondary responsibility; a 'C' if communication of the activity was necessary; a '+' if the rating needed extra emphasis; and the intersection should be left blank if there was no relationship between individual/department/supplier and task.

Maria was the best writer of the group, so she volunteered to take primary responsibility for communications. Roxanne volunteered to help Maria, so she received an 'S.' Ly volunteered to do the proofreading and needed to be in the "communication loop." So he was given a 'C' in the communication box. H.R. needed to keep in touch with everything going on, so they were also marked with a 'C'. The rest of the group was left blank in this category. The team continued until each intersection was identified and rated with a symbol or left blank (see Diagram #4.3)...

RESPONSIBILITY / TASK	Katherine	Raul	Roxanne	Maria	Ly	H.R.	Caterer
Food		S					P
Games		C	P				
Music	S				P		
Communications			S	P	C	C	
Prizes		P	C				
Decorations	P			S			
Pictures				S+	S	P	
Dunk Tanks	P					C	

Diagram #4.3 — Assign Strength Rating

Step 5:
Wrap up the Matrix Diagram Session

You know when to end the Matrix Diagram session when:

- All tasks have been identified.

- All individuals, groups, and suppliers have carried out the tasks that have been identified.

- Each intersection on the matrix has been rated.

- Action assignments have been made (i.e., communicate responsibilities, clarify responsibilities, etc.).

- You have thanked the participants.

After the team had rated all the intersections...

...they reviewed the Matrix Diagram to make sure that the assignments made sense and that everyone had time to carry out the tasks. The team then clarified exactly what each member would be doing in each task and set the first action assignments. Katherine thanked Raul, the recorder, and called for another meeting the following Wednesday to review progress, and make any necessary changes in responsibilities. She thanked the members of the team and then adjourned the meeting, confident that everything that needed to be done for the picnic would be taken care of and that everyone was clear on who was responsible for what.

Summary

In summary, use the Matrix Diagram when:

- You want to match tasks with the individuals, departments, or functions completing them. (Often when planning we forget or omit the actual writing of the plan. The Matrix Diagram forces team members to match tasks with the individuals, departments, or functions completing them.)

- You need to show a relationship between a task and the responsible person, department, or function. (The Matrix Diagram should become a working plan that shows every implementation step and the person or people responsible.)

- You want to assign accountability and plan actions. (Reviewing the Matrix Diagram periodically will help to hold people accountable to the plan of action.)

Chapter Four Review

List the five steps in the Matrix Diagram process:

1. _____

2. _____

3. _____

4. _____

5. _____

List the specific opportunities you have in your organization to use a Matrix Diagram.

_____

_____

_____

_____

_____

Choose one of the situations you listed above and complete the tasks and responsibilities sections in the Matrix Diagram below:

RESPONSIBILITY / TASK							

How can the Matrix Diagram help you with similar situations in the future?

_____

_____

_____

_____

Affinity Diagram

Chapter Objectives

In this chapter, you will learn to use the Affinity Diagram when:

☑ You want to add structure to a large or complicated issue.

☑ You want to break down a complicated issue into easy-to-understand categories.

☑ You want to gain agreement on an issue or situation.

Steps to follow when using the Affinity Diagram:

Step 1: State the Issue or Problem to be Worked On

Step 2: Generate Ideas for the Issue in Question (use index cards or sticky notes)

Step 3: Collect the Cards or Sticky Notes

Step 4: Arrange Cards/Sticky Notes into Related Groups

Step 5: Create a Title or Heading for Each Group

Step 6: Wrap Up the Affinity Session

In the following example, a team uses the Affinity Diagram to help organize a complex issue.

David is the leader of a cross-functional team...

...that has been asked to generate ideas that will reduce the cycle time in their service organization. David had seen the Affinity Diagram used in situations where large amounts of data needed to be organized. "Well," he decided, "this is certainly a situation where a tool like that could be helpful"...

Step 1:
State the Issue or Problem to be Worked On

At the start of your Affinity session:

- Provide a time limit for the session. Generally, 45-60 minutes is sufficient.

- Start with a clear, objective problem or goal statement that everyone agrees to.

After the group filed in,...

...David asked all those present to introduce themselves; then he announced the group's goal (which he had written on a flip chart). He also stated the meeting would last an hour...

Goal Statement:

Reducing Cycle Time

Step 2:
Generate Ideas for the Issue in Question

Each participant should think of ideas and write them on index cards, sticky notes, or have a recorder write them on a flip chart. (**Note:** *The advantage of using the flip chart is that everyone can see the ideas and build from them. The disadvantage of this technique is that group members may be intimidated by this process, and not participate.*)

51

The idea statements should be concisely listed in one to three words. (**Note:** *One idea per card or sticky note.*)

Form Product Release Team	*Shorter Approval Process*

David handed a stack of sticky notes...

...to each participant and asked them to write down their thoughts about reducing the cycle time in short, concise statements, one idea per sticky note. The group had trouble getting started; but, after a couple of minutes, all were busily writing. David gave the group 15 minutes to complete this part of the exercise...

Step 3:
Collect the Cards or Sticky Notes

Collect the cards (or sticky notes), mix them up; then spread them out (or stick them) on a flat surface.

David called "time,"...

...then collected the ideas from the participants. He mixed them up before sticking them on the wall to ensure the ideas would remain anonymous. That way no bias would be involved—all ideas would be treated the same...

Step 4:
Arrange Cards/Sticky Notes into Related Groups

All participants should pick out cards (or sticky notes) that list related ideas and set them aside. Repeat this until all of the cards (or sticky notes) have been placed in groupings.

After David stuck all the sticky notes to the wall...

...he asked the group to arrange the ideas into related groups (see Diagram #5.1). He asked that this be done in silence, so no one would be influenced by any other group member. As they began moving sticky notes around, it looked as though the ideas were being separated into four major groups...

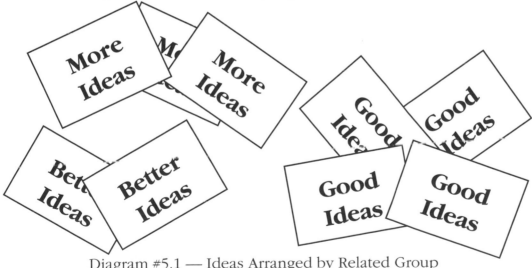

Diagram #5.1 — Ideas Arranged by Related Group

Note: *Don't force cards (or sticky notes) into groupings. There may be only one card (or sticky note) per grouping, or you may decide not to use the idea at all. Some ideas may be duplicates.*

This process should take about 15 minutes and works best when conversation between participants is not allowed. This encourages free thinking and discourages arguments over placement of cards/sticky notes.

Step 5:
Create a Title or Heading for Each Group

■ Develop a title or heading that best describes the theme of each group of cards (or sticky notes).

■ Headings should be short (one to three words) and describe the main theme/focus of the group it represents.

■ In order to see additional relationships, groups that are similar should be placed next to each other.

■ If groups are very similar, you can combine two or more groups to create one large group under a new title or heading.

■ Continue this process until there is agreement from the team on the grouping of cards.

After discussing the categorizing of ideas...

...for 15 minutes, it became obvious to the group that four very distinct categories of reductions were forming from the ideas on the sticky notes. The categories were data processing, procedures, service, and distribution. The remaining two sticky notes were grouped in a miscellaneous category (see Diagram #5.2)...

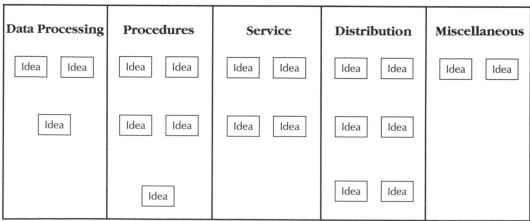

Data Processing	Procedures	Service	Distribution	Miscellaneous
Idea Idea	Idea Idea	Idea Idea	Idea Idea	Idea Idea
Idea	Idea Idea	Idea Idea	Idea Idea	
	Idea		Idea Idea	

Diagram #5.2 — Group the Ideas and Title Each Group

Step 6:
Wrap Up the Affinity Session

You know it's time to end the Affinity session when:

- Major groups have been identified.
- Assignments have been made to communicate and/or circulate the diagram to people outside the team for comments and ideas.
- You have thanked the participants.

Remember that the process of completing the Affinity Diagram is an ongoing one. It is likely the Diagram will be modified or changed.

For the first time in the organization's history...

...it was clear what could be done to reduce their cycle time. David was surprised by the number of ideas that were generated and by the potential impact they could bring to the organization. David asked Jennifer to circulate the final Affinity Diagram to the management team on Monday for their feedback and input.

He thanked the group for participating in the process and scheduled a follow-up meeting to discuss any changes to the Diagram and to identify ways to implement the ideas that were generated.

Summary

In summary, use the Affinity Diagram when:

- You want to add structure when handling a large or complicated issue (the Affinity Diagram is a structured method of Brainstorming that is used for larger, more complex activities such as developing a Mission Statement or a Vision Statement).

- You want to break down a complicated issue into easy-to-understand categories. (An issue or problem may have several sub-issues, or may be so large that it needs to be broken down into more manageable pieces.)

- You want to gain agreement on an issue or a situation. (When ideas are Brainstormed individually, the Affinity Diagram is a useful tool to ensure that all team members have an equal voice).

Chapter Five Review

When participants are arranging the cards or sticky notes into related groups, why is conversation discouraged?

_____

_____

_____

_____

What are the advantages of using the Affinity Diagram as a planning tool?

_____

_____

_____

_____

List the specific opportunities you have in your organization to use the Affinity Diagram.

_____

_____

_____

_____

Process Flow Chart

Chapter Objectives

In this chapter, you will learn to use the Process Flow Chart to:

- ☑ Define and analyze manufacturing, assembly or service processes.
- ☑ Build a step-by-step picture of the process for analysis, discussion, or communication purposes.
- ☑ Define, standardize, or find areas for improvement in a process.

The Process Flow Chart is a planning and analysis tool. It focuses on a specific function or activity, and does not allow for identification of various customers and suppliers. It's a more visual representation of a process, and is definitely more "systems-related."

Steps to follow when using a Process Flow Chart:

Step 1: Prepare for the Process Flow Chart Session

Step 2: Identify Major Process Tasks

Step 3: Draw the Process Flow Chart

Step 4: Analyze the Process Flow Chart

Having just completed...

...a Process Flow Chart class the week before, Marcus, a front desk supervisor at a large hotel, was anxious to try his new-found knowledge on a real "live" process. The hotel he worked for wanted to improve their quality of service by defining and evaluating their major service processes. Marcus and his team (Judy, Sharon, Alfonso, and Harold) had been charged with defining the guest check-in process for the company. And they were ready to get started...

Step 1:
Prepare for the Process Flow Charting Session

Prior to beginning your Process Flow Chart session:

- Create the Process Flow Chart symbol sheet. Your Process Flow Chart symbol sheet should show all of the flow chart symbols with corresponding explanations (see Diagram #6.1).

- Provide a time limit for the session. Creating the Process Flow Chart will likely take more than one session. Generally, a first session should last 50-60 minutes.

- Identify a recorder for the session. The job of the recorder is to draw the draft flow chart as the team identifies the steps and the appropriate symbols. The person you choose should have some knowledge of the Process Flow Chart procedure.

Note: *You may want to use sticky notes to help create the visual Process Flow Chart since changes may need to be made during the creation process.*

SYMBOL	NAME	EXPLANATION
	Elongated Circle	Shows the starting and ending points of a Process Flow Chart.
	Box	Any process task. Each box should contain a short description of the task being performed.
	Diamond	Any decision point. Each diamond should contain a question that can be answered *yes* or *no*.
	Connector	A small circle with a letter is used to connect one task of a flow chart to another.
	Document	A transfer *(or output)* of a hard copy document.
	Zigzag Arrow	Shows an electronic data transfer.
	Straight Arrow	Shows direction of process flow.

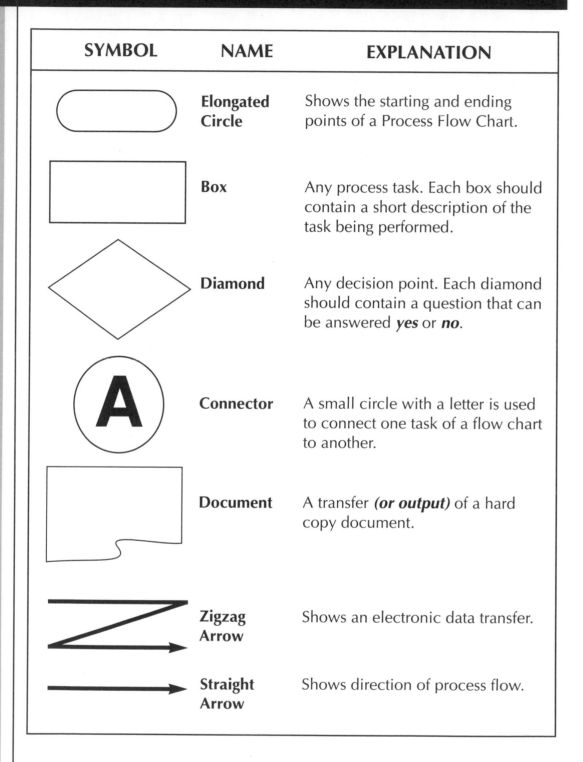

Diagram #6.1 — Flow Chart Symbols

Sharon, a manufacturing engineer...

...volunteered to be the recorder. Marcus posted the symbols they would use during the session (see Diagram #6.1). Sharon set the expectations for the meeting by saying, "In the next 60 minutes, let's identify the major tasks in the check-in process..."

Step 2:
Identify Major Process Tasks

Begin your Process Flow Chart session by identifying the first major task in the process you've chosen to analyze (this sets the boundary for the process). After this first task has been identified, ask questions to stimulate thought and to expedite the completion of the Process Flow Chart.

Some questions include:

Q. What really happens next in the process?

Q. Does a decision need to be made before the next task?

Q. What approvals are required before moving on to the next task?

Marcus said the group needed to answer...

...a few questions to make sure they came up with a true picture of the process. They needed to focus on what really happened in the process, instead of what was supposed to happen, what decisions and approvals were needed, and whether there was anything missing. Alfonso started by saying, "Well the first step is to see if they have a reservation, right?" Marcus' response was, "But don't we have to start even earlier in the process, say at the point where we greet the guest?" The group agreed and they had their first major task. Then Harold brought up a good point: "What if we greet the guest and they start yelling at us about having to wait in line?" Sharon listed the question as a decision for the flow chart. The group continued to list decisions and process tasks (see Diagram #6.2)...

Task	Major Process Tasks	Subtasks/Decisions	Symbol
1	Greet the guest	Good customer moment?	□ ◇
2	Check for reservation	If no reservation, check availability	□
3	Enter arrival details	Smoking preference correct?	□ ◇
		Bed size correct?	◇
		Length of stay correct?	◇
		Room rate correct?	◇
4	Enter credit card info and take imprint		□
5	Print confirmation agreement and have guest sign	Assistance needed? Call Bell Captain	◇ □
6	Wish guest a pleasant stay		□

Diagram #6.2 — List Process Tasks and Decisions

Step 3:
Draw the Process Flow Chart

Using the symbols identified in Step 1, draw the process tasks on flip chart paper or an overhead transparency. Every process will have a start and an end (shown by an elongated circle). In addition, all processes will have tasks (shown by a box), and most will have decision points (shown by a diamond). Decision points are yes or no questions that steer the process one way or another. Tasks may also be connected to other tasks using a connector (shown as a small circle with a letter). This particular symbol is used when you need to move to another task which may be several tasks away, rather than drawing long arrow lines.

After a lot of discussion and a few changes...

...the group agreed to the list of tasks and were ready to draw their flow chart. Sharon was elected as the resident artist and began by drawing the starting point (identified by the elongated circle) of their process. They agreed this was also the ending point of another flow chart—the one for greeting the guest at the door and assisting with car parking and luggage.

As they were completing the flow chart, Harold brought up something the others were all thinking too. "Looking at the process this way, we can really see where all the decisions are made because for one reason or another, we're not ready to go on to the next step." The group was getting anxious to look at ways to improve the process (see Diagram #6.3)...

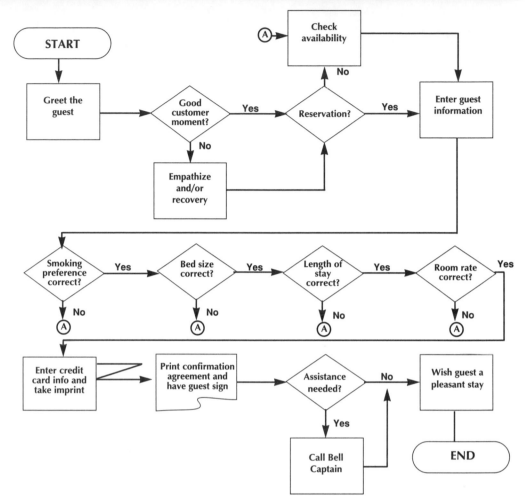

Diagram #6.3 — Draw the Flow Chart

Step 4:
Analyze the Process Flow Chart

The Process Flow Chart offers many opportunities for process analysis.
These opportunities include analyses of:

- Time per event (reducing cycle time)
- Process repeats (preventing rework)
- Duplication of effort (identifying and eliminating duplicate tasks)
- Unnecessary tasks (eliminating tasks that are in the process for no apparent reason)
- Value-added vs. non-value-added tasks

"Value-Added"

Tasks within your work process that contribute to the ability to meet and/or exceed your customers' requirements are termed *value-added*. These include activities that reduce errors, or tasks that decrease the cycle time of a work process, such as:

Value-Added
☐ Improve processes
■ Making "front line" decisions
☐ Defining measurements
☐ Making action plans
■ Reviewing progress
☐ Analyzing successes and failures
☐ Providing feedback to suppliers
☐ Meeting with customers
■ Setting goals

"Non-Value-Added"

Tasks within your work process that do not contribute to the ability to meet and/or exceed your customers' requirements are termed *non-value-added*. These include tasks that are unnecessary or increase the cycle time of a work process, such as:

Non-Value-Added
☐ Fixing errors without knowing root cause
☐ Getting numerous approvals
☐ Duplicating work and reports
☐ Waiting for materials or direction
☐ Collecting non-relevant data
☐ Writing reports that are not read
☐ Going to non-productive meetings
☐ Reworking other people's outputs
☐ Waiting for further instructions

"A Process Flow Chart analysis will uncover any indication of loss or waste."

Each type of analysis listed has the potential to save individuals, departments, or companies varying amounts of time (which translates into money), because a Process Flow Chart analysis will uncover any indication of loss or waste.

Before you make any process changes, though, you'll increase your analysis power if you first measure your current performance. This measurement will serve as a baseline to determine if the changes you made to the process have had a positive effect.

At the beginning of the next meeting...

...Marcus said, "Let's look at the flow chart and see what we can learn from it." The group spent the remaining time discussing potential process problems and areas for improvement (i.e., unnecessary steps or process redundancies). Kenny stated that by identifying and eliminating unnecessary steps, time could be reduced and customer satisfaction increased (see Diagram #6.3).

"What about all these decision steps where we confirm the customer's room arrangements? Maybe we can't eliminate those steps, but we should be able to make it a lot easier," began Harold. Sharon continued, "Yes, and maybe we could get the reservations department to change a couple of things they do, so we have more information on the same computer screen." The group then started to look at ways to reduce or eliminate non-value-added tasks...

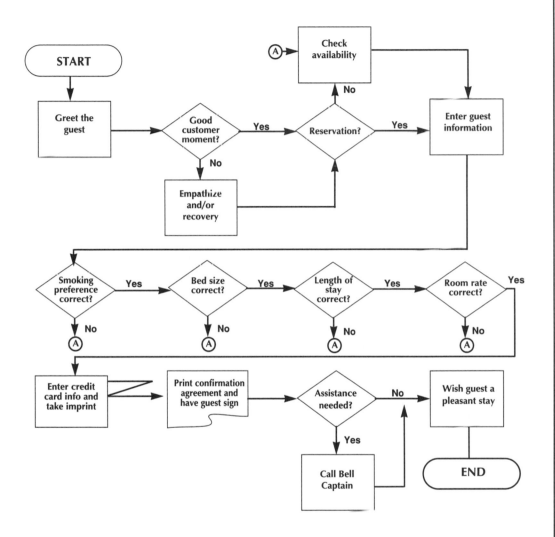

Diagram #6.3 — Draw the Flow Chart

Follow Up:
Decide on Next Steps

Analyzing the Process Flow Chart is not the end of the procedure. To fully utilize this effective tool, you need to determine what to do with your analysis.

Additional steps can include:

- Distributing the flow chart for review.
- Creating measurements based on the process analysis.
- Changing the process based on customer information and collected data.
- Concluding that changes will not be cost-effective.

After completing an initial analysis of the process...

...Sharon volunteered to take the flip chart information and make a printout for all managers to review. Marcus said, "We should focus our next meeting around problem areas, or areas for improvement (i.e., unnecessary steps or process redundancies)." Harold suggested that the group collect customer information about internal and external customer requirements. Alfonso suggested using a survey he had created.

The ideas were coming fast and furious, so Judy used the flip chart to record the "action items." Marcus was pleased with the team's performance and was excited about the possibility of improvements. The Process Flow Chart really did make a difference.

Summary

In summary, use the Process Flow Chart when:

- You are working with a service-, manufacturing-, or assembly-related process. The Process Flow Chart may be more appropriate when focusing on a specific function or task, and when the identification of various customers and suppliers is not crucial.

- You and your team need to define the tasks in a process.

- You are trying to determine areas for improvement in a process. The Process Flow Chart will help you and your team identify process redundancies and other problem areas.

- You are designing a new process. The Process Flow Chart will provide a visual representation of the process.

- You are standardizing an existing process. The Process Flow Chart will clarify differing viewpoints concerning the activity in a process.

Chapter Six Review

List the four major steps in completing a Process Flow Chart.

1. _____

2. _____

3. _____

4. _____

Match the following flow chart symbols to the appropriate explanations.

_____ Any process task. Should contain a short description of the task being performed.

_____ A transfer (or output) of a hard copy document.

_____ Shows the starting and ending points of a Process Flow Chart.

_____ Any decision point. Should contain a question that can be answered "yes" or "no."

List three opportunities the Process Flow Chart offers for process analysis:

_____

_____

_____

What specific opportunities do you have in your organization to use
Process Flow Charts?

_____

_____

_____

What would you be analyzing in the process (i.e., time involved,
redundancies, repeats, etc.)?

_____

_____

_____

_____

Histogram

Chapter Objectives

In this chapter, you will learn to use the Histogram to:

☑ Communicate information about variation in a process.

☑ Make decisions on the focus of improvement efforts.

Steps to follow when using a Histogram:

Step 1: Gather and Tabulate the Data
Step 2: Calculate the Range and Interval Width
Step 3: Draw the Horizontal and Vertical Axes
Step 4: Tabulate the Data by Intervals
Step 5: Plot the Data
Step 6: Analyze the Histogram

The example that follows shows how a team used the Histogram to analyze variation in the time it took to process a purchase order requisition.

Alex had heard it before...

...and enough was enough! As one of the specialists in purchasing, he had heard several complaints about how long it took his department to process purchase order requisitions. When he looked at the figures for the past few quarters, the records showed the average processing turnaround time varied only slightly from an average of 4.5 days, an acceptable average time. Alex brought the issue up with Phyllis, the department head. Her response was, "You're right, the average hasn't changed, but maybe there's something going on that isn't showing up." Along with Beth, another specialist in the department, they decided to look closely at the variation. Beth suggested creating a Histogram to compare actual turnaround times...

In the ideal process, variation is minimized and under control. This situation is reflected in a Histogram showing a normal, symmetric distribution, or "bell-shaped" curve. Most of the measurements fall near the center, with roughly equal numbers falling on either side of the center point (see Diagram #7.1).

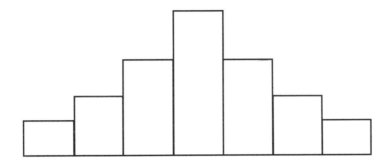

Diagram #7.1 — Histogram of a Norm Distribution

The width of each column represents an interval, or group, of observations within a range, while the height represents the number of observations falling within a given interval.

Step 1:
Gather and Tabulate the Data

Histograms are often used to group measures, such as time, weight, size, frequency of a certain occurrence, etc., into clusters (or intervals) around an average of observations.

The clues given by the Histogram lie in its shape; specifically the height of the bars and patterns of the bars relative to each other.

The more data used to calculate the average, the more accurate your Histogram will be. Try to get 40 to 50 observations over a predetermined period of time (a week, a month, etc.) if you can.

"The more data used to calculate the average, the more accurate your Histogram will be."

73

Alex and Beth reviewed the data...

...for the last month and discovered 42 purchase orders had been processed. The average turnaround time was exactly what it was for the quarter — 4.5 days. They transferred the data from the department's files to a data sheet in order to have all the numbers in one place (see Diagram #7.2)...

Number of Days Required to Process Each Purchase Order (last month)

2.75	3.5	4.25	8	8.25	4
2.5	5.75	2	3	3.25	4.75
3.5	4.5	3.75	7.25	5.25	4.25
2.25	1.5	7.25	3.75	4.25	5.5
6	4.5	8	4.75	5	2
6.25	4	8.5	4.25	2.5	4.75
3.25	4.5	1.75	6.5	3.25	4.25

Diagram #7.2 — Tabulated Data for Histogram

Step 2:
Calculate the Range and Interval Width

Before you can begin to plot the data, set up a scale and decide on the intervals for the data.

Calculate the range:
Simply calculate the difference between the lowest and highest numbers in the data collected (e.g., if the highest number in the data is 22.5 inches and the lowest is 12.2 inches, the range would be 10.3 inches).

Calculate the interval width:

Decide how many bars you want to show on the Histogram. Usually 6 to 12 work best. Then divide the range by the number of bars to determine the width of an interval. Each interval represents a bar on the Histogram. In the above example, the interval width would be 1.3 inches if you were going to use eight bars (10.4 inches divided by 8), or 1.04 inches if you were going to use 10 bars (10.4 divided by 10).

Beth and Alex calculated the range...

...of data from the table. They decided to use a seven-day period. They thought about using only 7 bars for the Histogram, equaling an interval width of one day, but decided to use 14, giving them a width of .5 days (see Diagram #7.3). Beth felt the additional breakdown of data would give them a clearer picture of the situation...

Range = 22.5 - 12.2 = 10.3 Inches

Interval Width = 1.3 inches (10.4 ÷ 8)

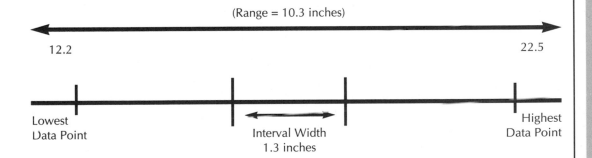

(Range = 10.3 inches)

12.2   22.5

Lowest
Data Point

Interval Width
1.3 inches

Highest
Data Point

Diagram #7.3 — Calculating the Range and Interval Width

Step 3:
Draw the Horizontal and Vertical Axes

Draw the horizontal axis. Plot intervals on this axis using previously calculated interval widths.

Draw the vertical axis. Select the highest point for the axis by dividing the number of observations by three and using the resulting number (i.e., if you had 60 observations, your scale for the vertical axis would go up to 20).

To simplify things...

...Alex set the scale for the vertical axis at 14 (42 divided by 3). He looked at the table and realized none of the numbers ever came close to showing up 14 times, so he lowered the scale to 10 (see Diagram #7.4). "That should do it," he thought and finished drawing the two axes on the graph paper...

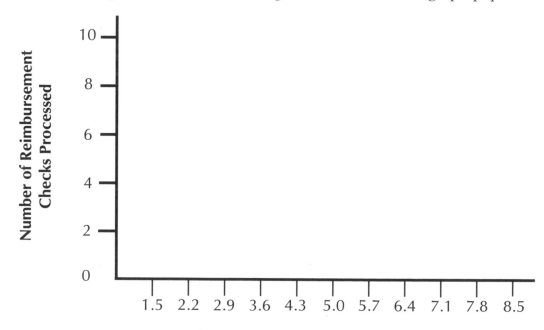

Diagram #7.4 — Draw the Horizontal and Vertical Axes

Step 4:
Tabulate the Data by Intervals

In order to plot the bars on a Histogram, organize observations and group them into intervals.

Setting up the table...

...to organize the data by intervals was a breeze, thought Alex. Beth called out the number from the original data table and he made tick marks in the new table. "Now, all we need to do is draw the bars on the Histogram to these hcights and we'll be finished," said Alex. Beth called out the last number (see Diagram #7.5)...

Interval	Number of Observations
1.5 — 2.2	I I I I
2.2 — 2.9	I I I I
2.9 — 3.6	⊬⊬ I
3.6 — 4.3	⊬⊬ I I I I
4.3 — 5.0	⊬⊬ I
5.0 — 6.4	I I I
5.7 — 6.4	I I I
6.4 — 7.1	I
7.1 — 7.8	I I
7.8 — 8.5	I I I I

Diagram #7.5 — Tabulating the Data by Intervals

Step 5:
Plot the Data

Once the intervals have been determined and the data has been categorized according to how many of the measurers fall within each interval, the next step is to plot the data on the Histogram.

Simply draw the bars for each interval. The height of each bar represents the number of measures corresponding to its interval on the horizontal axis.

With pencil in hand...

...Beth began drawing bars on the Histogram, beginning with the four observations for the first interval of 1.5 to 2.2, and continuing to the four observations for the last interval of 7.8 to 8.5. "The shape of our Histogram doesn't look right," said Beth. "The data should be grouped tightly around the center, shouldn't it?" (see Diagram #7.6)...

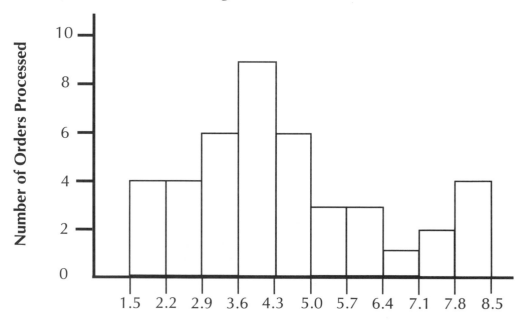

Diagram #7.6 — Drawing the Bars

Step 6:
Analyze the Histogram

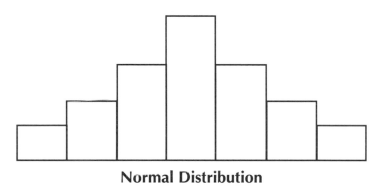

Normal Distribution

Analyze the Histogram to find out what is happening in your process. The example above illustrates normal distribution. Most of the measurements are concentrated in the middle intervals, indicating variation from the average is under control and manageable.

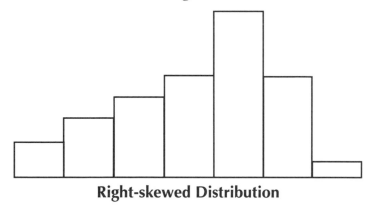

Right-skewed Distribution

The second Histogram shows a process which is skewed to the right. This indicates something is happening in the process to produce more measures on the higher end of the scale than on the lower end. This is caused by inconsistencies in the process, such as a new employee taking longer to complete a task (if completion time is the measure), inconsistent procedures, and so on.

When your Histogram shows a left or right skew, track the data points on the skewed end to find what the common patterns (or potential causes) are.

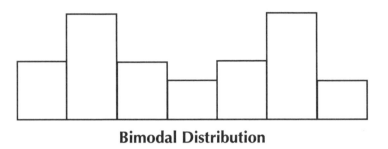

Bimodal Distribution

The third Histogram illustrates a process with clusters of measures on opposite ends of the scale (bimodal distribution). This indicates serious inconsistencies in a process. Using the average to measure the performance of the process is virtually meaningless, since most of the measures occur well above or below the average.

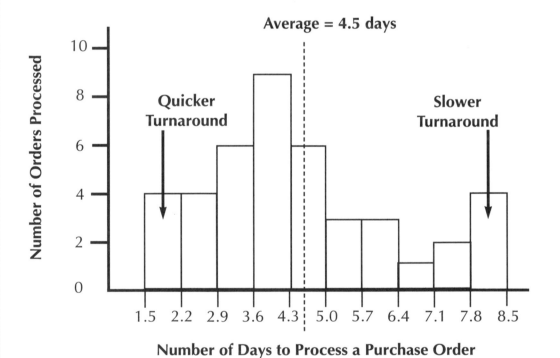

Diagram #7.7 — Analyzing the Histogram

The Histogram...

...showed an interesting pattern (see Diagram #7.7). The average time had already been calculated as 4.5 days (the total of the times divided by 42 observations for the month). The Histogram showed the largest grouping in the interval of 3.6 to 4.3 days, which was close to the average, and made sense.

"But why are the bars getting higher for the last two intervals, between 7.1 days and 8.5 days?" asked Beth. "If it wasn't for those intervals, our average would be lower. Why do some purchase orders take that long to process anyway?"

"I think I know what is going on here," replied Phyllis. "The Histogram should be tapering off to the left side too, but it doesn't. 'Rush' requests from some managers account for the P.O.'s being turned around in a day or two. That explains the relatively high number in the interval of 1.5 to 2.2 days. When we deal with those special cases, we have to set aside someone else's request, holding it up for a couple of days—that's what may be showing up on the right side of the Histogram."

"So we may be receiving complaints about slow turnaround because of the special treatment we give to purchase orders for certain managers who have rush requests, right?" asked Alex.

Follow Up:
Agree on Next Steps

After you have analyzed your Histogram, you might find yourself in one of the following situations:

■ Your analysis has produced useful answers. You've learned what is happening in your process, and why the variation occurs in a certain way (i.e., a skewed, bimodal, or other abnormal distribution shows up in your Histogram). As a result, you need to reduce the variation to a target level and decide when to plot the next Histogram (in order to track progress).

■ The Histogram's shape provided clues about the type of variation occurring. It is skewed to the right, meaning the variation is occurring mainly on that end of your measurement scale. You have an idea about what's behind the picture, but can't put your finger on the precise underlying cause. In this case, you need to dig deeper to find out what is really going on.

■ You are not sure what the clues are behind the Histogram's shape. In this case, it is a good idea to bring others into the picture. Ask for their help in analyzing why the data is skewed, bimodal, or any other abnormal shape.

Summary

In summary, use a Histogram when:

■ You want to verify or investigate whether a problem really exists. The Histogram serves as an indicator of a problem, and further investigation can verify the source or cause of the problem.

■ You want a tool to communicate distribution of data, or to create a "picture" of variation within a process. Using a Histogram when working together as a group is a very effective way of ensuring a common understanding of the information.

■ You want to track changes in process variation across time (i.e., by using your initial Histogram as a baseline, and creating new ones to measure changes as you improve the underlying process).

Chapter Seven Review

What specific opportunities do you have in your organization to use Histograms?

_____

_____

_____

What types of data and measures would be needed to create these Histograms?

_____

_____

_____

How many observations would you gather?

_____

_____

_____

What tools would be appropriate to further analyze the situation, if necessary?

_____

_____

_____

Run Chart

Chapter Objectives

In this chapter, you will learn to use a Run Chart to:

- ☑ Collect and interpret data.
- ☑ Create a picture of what is happening in the situation you are analyzing.
- ☑ Find patterns yielding valuable insights.
- ☑ Compare one period of data to another, checking for changes.

The Run Chart is a type of line graph used as an analysis tool. It tracks changes in the variable being measured over a period of time to identify patterns.

Steps to follow when using a Run Chart:

Step 1: Determine What to Measure

Step 2: Draw the Graph

Step 3: Plot the Data

The example that follows shows how one professional used the Run Chart to verify a hunch.

Dianna, Manager of the Telephone Customer Service Department...

...realized that the department was not meeting their goal of answering calls within 30 seconds. Her reports were showing that the average response time was gradually creeping higher. Dianna felt that a clear pattern was developing, but she needed to collect and interpret more data to find out what was going on. She had used a Run Chart in the past. This seemed like the perfect opportunity to use it again...

Step 1:
Determine What to Measure

The first step in constructing a Run Chart is selecting one key measure to track over a period of time. This measure should be a "quality/productivity" (external customer or internal process) indicator that will provide useful information for making decisions.

Note: *Measures can also be tracked against other bases, such as production batches, shifts, and so on.*

Possible measures include:

- Volume (i.e., how much over a specified period of time)
- Cycle time (i.e., how long something takes)
- Errors (i.e., how many are incorrect over a period of time)
- Waste (i.e., how much is reworked or rejected)

After you have determined what to measure, decide on the period of time during which you will collect data. Possible time intervals include hourly, daily, weekly, monthly, quarterly, etc.

Dianna determined that her quality measure...

...would be "average seconds to answer phone calls." She decided to start with a daily measurement, but realized that the measurement may have to be changed to hourly at some point in the future...

Step 2:
Draw the Graph

Drawing the graph consists of three simple steps:

- Name the graph. The name should describe what you are measuring and the time duration you've chosen.

■ Draw the vertical axis. The measure is always on the vertical axis, and is shown in number of occurrences or percentages.

■ Draw the horizontal axis. The time interval or other measurement base is always shown on the horizontal axis and is spaced equally apart (see Diagram #8.1).

With the quality measurement chosen...

...and the time interval determined, the rest was a breeze. Dianna named the graph — Customer Service Response Time for August — and then drew the vertical and horizontal axes. She labeled the vertical axis, "Average Response Time (seconds)," and the horizontal axis, "Days in August"...

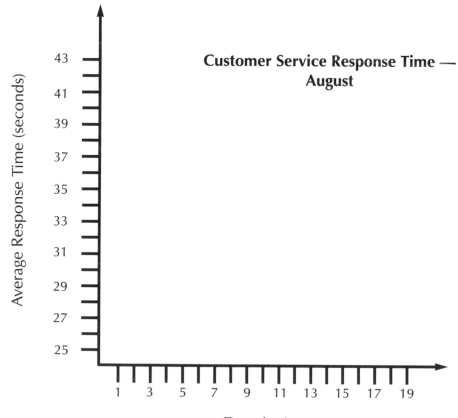

Diagram #8.1 — Draw the Run Chart

Step 3:
Plot the Data

Collect data for your chosen measurement. Each data point should then be plotted on the graph in the appropriate location given its level of occurrence (or percentage) and time interval. If you connect the points, it'll be easier to interpret the graph. Finally, calculate the average occurrence or percentage and plot that on the graph. The average line will help you to see abnormalities in the process condition (i.e., something other than random points around the average line).

Follow these tips for collecting and plotting data:

- Plot data points in the order they occur.
- Collect data on a regular basis (i.e., get into a habit of collecting data at the same time, and storing it in the same place).
- Evaluate data on a regular basis (i.e., post data in a place where it can be seen and reviewed by customers and suppliers).

As the days in August went by,...

...Dianna continued to plot data on her Run Chart. The employees in her department began to take interest in the chart as the month progressed, because they could finally see that average response time was more than they had previously thought. Dianna was careful to plot the response time as it occurred, thus ensuring the accuracy of the measurement. She also connected the data points to help her see both the trends and the extreme levels of variation in the amount of response time (see Diagram #8.2)...

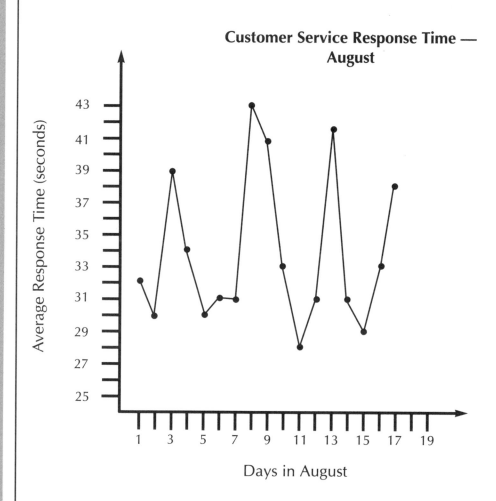

Diagram #8.2 — Plot the Data

Decide on next steps

Once you've plotted the graph, you have the option to do one or more of the following:

- Search for patterns in the data (i.e., errors are higher on Tuesday during the second shift).

- Determine the root cause of the error (i.e., a new employee is working Tuesday's second shift, and has not been trained yet).

- Investigate extreme highs or lows in data points (extreme variation around the average line indicates opportunity for improvement).

- Continue measuring to track the effect of changes (i.e., you can prove that the changes are working by tracking the data).

- Create a Control Chart to provide more information about process variation and control.

At the end of the month...

...Dianna calculated the average response time and drew the line on the graph. Her original hunch seemed correct. A pattern was developing, and she decided to continue collecting the data to further verify it. Also present were some extreme highs and lows in the data points on the graph (see Diagram #8.3). This looked unusual to Dianna, so she decided her next step would involve converting the Run Chart to a Control Chart (see Chapter 10 — Control Chart). That way she could discover whether the increased response time was normal or whether something truly unusual was taking place.

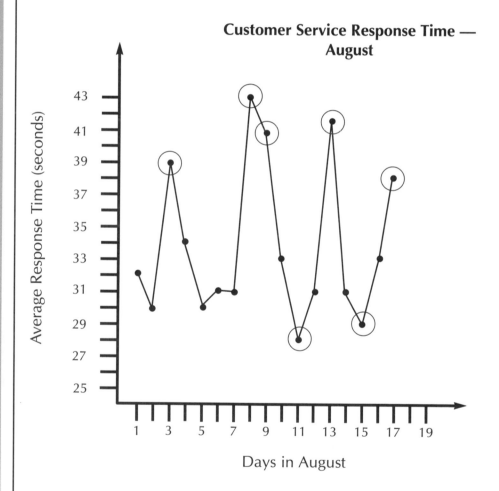

Diagram #8.3 — Interpret Data

Summary

In summary, use the Run Chart when:

- Trying to show trends in measurements over time or comparison from one measurement base to another (such as different shifts, teams, production runs, etc.). Since the Run Chart is always based on some comparable measurement such as time, comparison of data is quick and easy.

- You need to check for long-term changes. Often data changes slowly over time. The Run Chart, if regularly updated, will show overall changes in the process average which may indicate process instability.

- You want to show process variations. The Run Chart will help you spot extremes in process variation.

- You want to evaluate changes made to the process. After improvements have been made to the process, continue to collect data using the Run Chart to verify the effectiveness of the change.

"Since the Run Chart is always based on some comparable measurement such as time, comparison of data is quick and easy."

91

Chapter Eight Review

On which Run Chart axis should the quality/productivity measure be placed?

_____Vertical _____Horizontal

On which Run Chart axis should the time interval (or other measurement base) be placed?

_____Vertical _____Horizontal

What specific opportunities do you have in your organization to use Run Charts?

_____

_____

_____

_____

Would these situations involve tracking certain measures across time or some other base?

Time (___daily, ____weekly, ____monthly)

Batches or runs

Work teams (such as shifts, geographical units, etc.)

Other bases (specify): _____

Which measures would be appropriate for these situations?

_____

_____

_____

_____

Run Charts are always based on comparable measurements.

True or False

Run Charts will not show overall change in the process average if regularly updated.

True or False

Pareto Chart

Chapter Objectives

In this chapter, you will learn to use a Pareto Chart when:

☑ Determining the relative frequency or importance of different problems or causes.

☑ Focusing on vital issues by ranking problems and causes in terms of significance.

Note: *Before you can construct a Pareto Chart, you need to know how to use Check Sheets (since the data you collect with the Check Sheet will be used to construct the Pareto Chart; see Chapter 1) and other basic data-gathering tools.*

Steps to follow when using a Pareto Chart:

Step 1: Identify the Categories of Problems, or Causes to be Compared

Step 2: Select a Standard Unit of Measurement and the Time Period to be Studied

Step 3: Collect and Summarize Data

Step 4: Draw the Horizontal and Vertical Axes

Step 5: Plot the Bars on the Pareto Chart

The example that follows illustrates how the Pareto Chart is used to help distinguish opinion from fact.

Ursula, administration supervisor in the mail room...

...had been hearing from the company's internal customers about frequent late and wrong mail delivered by her department, and she wanted the "problems" corrected. Ursula and Louis, an administrative assistant, decided that constructing a Pareto Chart would help them pinpoint the specific problems and their cause(s)...

Step 1:
Identify the Categories of Problems or Causes to be Compared

Begin by organizing the problems or causes into a handful of categories. Narrow down a long list to a manageable number of eight categories or less.

For example, if you are measuring reasons why you were late to work over a period of time, possible categories could consist of too busy, traffic, oversleeping, arguing with your spouse or children, etc.

Ursula called together a small group of people...

...who had been on the receiving end of some of the mail room's errors. She asked them to brainstorm a list of errors they had noticed in the last few months. Ursula then asked the group to identify five error categories. The categories chosen included mail runs behind schedule, receiving wrong mail, outgoing mail delivered to the post office late, rude mail clerks, and incorrect charges...

Step 2:
Select a Standard Unit of Measurement and the Time Period to be Studied

The measurement you select will depend on the type of situation you are working with. It could be a measure of how often something occurs (such as defects, errors, overflows, cost overruns, etc.), how often reasons are cited in surveys as the cause of a given effect, or a specific measurement of volume size.

- ■ **Time**
- ■ **Defects**
- ■ **Frequency**
- ■ **Size**

Note: When selecting a sample time period, allow a long enough span to gather the required data. For example, if you were measuring reasons why people get to work late, you would not use data gathered from just one day of the week. On Monday, traffic might be heavier than Tuesday or Wednesday. By spanning a week or more, any special cases such as Monday morning traffic, will balance out against the other reasons why people are late to work.

"Allow a long enough span to gather the required data."

Ursula gave Louis the go-ahead...

...to collect data and build the Pareto Chart. Louis had been in a training session the month before, where he learned he had to measure the right variable if the chart was to give them any valid insights. He began tracking all complaints in a 30-day span—a long enough period to get a clear picture of what was going on. Louis realized the internal customers were not reporting all the errors to the mail room. He personally contacted each customer, requesting they report all problems. Louis even mailed each customer special cards to record this information. When he explained to them the information gathered would reduce errors, the customers were only too happy to help!...

Step 3:
Collect and Summarize Data

Begin by creating a three-column table for which the headings should be "error category," "frequency," and "percent of total." The items in the "error category" column should include the different types of errors (or causes of errors) that occur. This information can be taken directly from your Check Sheet.

Under the "frequency" column, write in the totals for each of the categories.

Now divide each number in the "frequency" column by the total number of measurements. This will give you the percentage of the total. For example, if the frequency for a given category is 30, and the total measurements add up to 80, the percentage (30/80) equals 37.5%. Write your calculated percentage for each category under the heading entitled "Percent of Total."

Louis started by creating a table...

...for the data he had collected during the past month (see Diagram #9.1). He listed the various complaints made under the category column. Louis then recorded the frequency of each error in the second column (this information was obtained directly from the Check Sheet). Finally he calculated the percentage of total complaints for each of the categories and recorded those in the appropriate spaces. Louis was now ready to draw his Pareto Chart...

Error Category	Frequency	Percent of Total
Behind Schedule	7	16%
Wrong Deliveries	20	44%
Late P.O.	12	27%
Rude Clerks	1	2%
Incorrect Charges	5	11%
TOTAL	45	100%

Diagram #9.1 — Create a Data Table

Step 4:
Draw the Horizontal and Vertical Axes

Begin by drawing the horizontal axis. Draw a line from left to right on a piece of paper. Make the line long enough so that all the categories can be written under it. Write the categories in descending order with the most frequently occurring category on the far left (or beginning of the horizontal line). Label the axis. The label should tell the readers what they are looking at (i.e., causes for being late to work, types of customer complaints, etc.).

Next draw a vertical line up from the far left point of the horizontal axis. This line will indicate the frequencies for each of the categories. Scale it so the value at the top of the axis is slightly higher than the highest frequency number. Label this axis also. Again, the label should tell the readers what they are looking at (i.e., frequency of occurrence), and be located just to the left of the frequency numbers.

Louis drew the horizontal and vertical axes...

...and labeled the horizontal axis "Error Category," and the vertical axis "Frequency of Occurrence." Since schedules were the complaint occurring most frequently, Louis made "Behind Schedule" the first category on the far left. He wrote in "Wrong Deliveries" as the next category on the axis, and so on (see Diagram #9.2)...

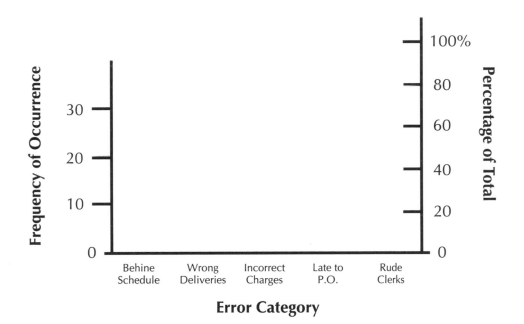

Diagram #9.2 — Organize the Pareto Chart

Draw another vertical axis, this time from the far right side of the horizontal axis. This line will represent the percentage scale and should be scaled so that the point for the number of occurrences on the left matches with the corresponding percentage on the right.

Step 5:
Plot the Bars on the Pareto Chart

The final step is to plot the data by drawing a series of bars in decreasing height from left to right (see Diagram #9.3).

Note: *Categories with very few items can be combined into an "Other" or "Miscellaneous" category, which is placed on the extreme right of the last bar.*

To plot the cumulative line, place a dot above each bar at a height corresponding to the scale on the right vertical axis. Starting with the first column on the left, draw a line to connect these dots from left to right, ending with the 100% point at the top of the right vertical axis.

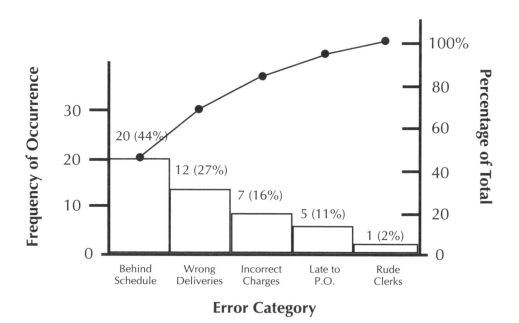

Diagram #9.3 — Plot the Data

While Louis plotted the chart...

...the biggest issues became clear. Two sources, schedules missed and wrong deliveries, accounted for 71% of the problem. Louis and Ursula decided to create a game plan before presenting the chart to the rest of the department...

Follow Up:
Decide on the Next Steps

You now have an easy-to-read and understand chart that should help you decide what to tackle first. While working on your problems (i.e., customer complaints, etc.), however, continue to investigate. For example, just because a certain problem occurs most often doesn't necessarily mean it demands your greatest attention. Also consider the following:

■ What makes the biggest difference to the customer?

■ What will it cost to correct this problem?

■ What will it cost if we don't correct this problem?

Investigating all the angles will help you decide which problem should be worked on first.

Remember that while your data will lead you in a certain direction, the customer should have the final say on what should be corrected first. Continue to collect and plot data to verify your original findings, and also to evaluate any changes (improvements) you make.

> **"Just because a certain problem occurs most often doesn't necessarily mean it demand your greatest attention."**

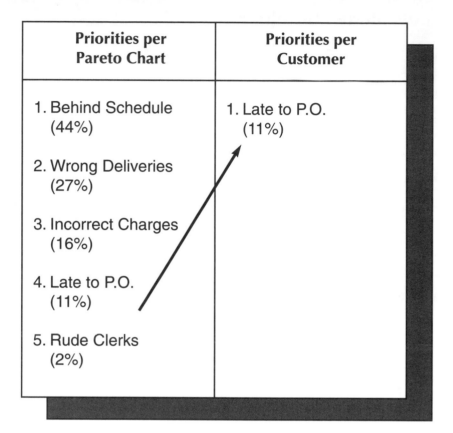

Priorities per Pareto Chart	Priorities per Customer
1. Behind Schedule (44%)	1. Late to P.O. (11%)
2. Wrong Deliveries (27%)	
3. Incorrect Charges (16%)	
4. Late to P.O. (11%)	
5. Rude Clerks (2%)	

Having completed his Pareto Chart...

...Louis reviewed the data with Ursula and agreed to share it with a cross section of the mail room's internal customers. This meeting provided new insight. The number one complaint for several of the key customers was mail not being delivered to the post office on time. This error did not happen often, but when it did, customers experienced severe problems (i.e., mail not received at the intended destination in time).

Louis discovered firsthand that although the data highlighted one finding (i.e., schedules are the biggest problem), the customers' perspective was completely different (i.e., "get the mail to the post office on time"). Based on this information, Louis, Ursula, and a cross-section of the Mail Room employees and internal customers created an improvement team to focus on delivering mail to the post office on time. They decided to tackle this objective first before moving on to missed schedules.

Summary

In summary, use the Pareto Chart when:

- You or your team need to select a problem or process to improve (i.e., the problem occurs most often). Remember the most frequent problem isn't necessarily the problem that should be worked on.

- You or your team need to evaluate improvement efforts that you have already made (to show if things are improving or not).

- You or your team want to identify the distribution of the cause(s) of a problem (i.e., which variable causes are what percent of the problem).

Chapter Nine Review

List the five steps of creating a Pareto Chart.

1. _____

2. _____

3. _____

4. _____

5. _____

For what two general reasons would you use a Pareto Chart?

_____

_____

_____

_____

What opportunity do you have in your organization to use Pareto Charts?

_____

_____

_____

_____

What needs to be measured to gather the necessary data?

_____

_____

_____

_____

How might the Pareto Chart help make decisions and communicate to others the specific situations you identified above?

Situation: _____

Making Decisions	*Communicate to Others*
_____	_____
_____	_____
_____	_____
_____	_____

Control Chart

Chapter Objectives

In this chapter, you will learn to use the Control Chart to:

☑ Interpret data about a process by creating a picture of the boundaries of acceptable variation.

☑ Objectively determine if a process is "in control" or "out of control."

Variation is part of everyday life, and no less so in the workplace. For example, there is variation in the length of time it takes to complete a form, and variation in the weight and volume of tangible products, etc.

Regardless of whether you need to track variation in a manufacturing process or a service environment, Control Charts are a useful tool for setting boundaries on the variation within a process. They show you when these boundaries are overstepped, and you can then look for clues to the causes.

Note: *There are many types of Control Charts. This chapter and example cover the P-Chart (i.e., percent defective) only.*

Steps to follow when using a Control Chart:

Step 1: Determine What to Measure

Step 2: Collect the Data

Step 3: Plot the Data

Step 4: Calculate the Control Limits

Step 1:
Determine What to Measure

The first step in constructing a Control Chart is identical to the first step in creating a Run Chart. Identify one key measurement that you want to track over time, or other base measurement appropriate for your situation. This measurement should be a "quality/productivity" (external customer or internal process) indicator that will provide information useful in making decisions.

Possible measures include:

- Volume (i.e., how much over a specified period of time)
- Cycle time (i.e., how long something takes)
- Errors (i.e., how many are incorrect over a period of time)
- Waste (i.e., how much is reworked or rejected)

The following example illustrates how you can use the Control Chart in a service-related situation.

A medium-sized wholesale distributor of pharmaceutical drugs...

...recently embarked on a quality-improvement effort. Dave, the new quality manager, discovered through a customer survey that the billing process was rated "high" in importance and received the most complaints. He decided to collect data on the number and types of errors to determine if the billing process was "in control" (i.e., its variation was due to day-to-day or common causes of variation) and to see where improvements could be made. Dave decided to use a P-chart, which would identify the percentage of billing statements that contained errors...

Step 2:
Collect the Data

Collect data for your measurement by using the form provided (see the Appendix) or by creating your own. Then calculate the percent defective in the space provided. Items to be included on your data collection form include, but are not limited to:

- **Date**
- **Number Inspected**
- **Number Defective**
- **Types of Defects**
- **Percent Defective**

Some tips that will help you collect data include:

- Use a sample of at least 50 items (the sample should be big enough to give an average of three or more defects per sample).

- Avoid taking samples over long periods of time (i.e., try to break large samples up into more manageable two- or four-hour time periods versus sampling a full 24-hour day).

- Avoid varying sample sizes.

- Take a minimum of 20 sets of samples.

The billing department...

...had completed basic statistics training, so it wasn't difficult for Dave to find volunteers eager to test their newly acquired skills. Laura, a billing analyst, offered to inspect 50 invoices on a daily basis to find out how many times customers were being billed at the wrong price (the number one complaint). Dave asked her to use the data collection form to keep track of the information that would be used to determine the state of the billing process. (see Diagram #10.1).

Remarks	Date	# Inspected	Wrong Price	Wrong Quantity	Wrong Address	Incomplete Information	% Defective
			Types of Defects				
	7-14	50	8	1	1		20
	7-15	50	13			1	28
	7-16	50	11		1		24
	7-17	50	10	3	1	1	30
	7-18	50	12		1	1	28
	7-21	50	14				30
	7-22	50	9	3	2	1	15
	7-23	50	35	12		2	48
	7-24	50	19		1	1	22

Diagram #10.1 — Sample Control Chart Data Collection Sheet

Note: *This is a partial chart of the data Laura collected.*

Step 3:
Plot the Data

After you've taken at least 20 samples and calculated the percent defective for each, create the plotting scale on the vertical axis of the graph. The scale should reveal whatever is appropriate for your particular measurement. Create a horizontal axis with a point for each sample date.

Plot the individual percent defectives on the graph. Next, compute the average percent defective by adding all of the percent defectives for the individual samples and dividing the results by the total number of samples taken (in this case 20). Draw a horizontal line at the appropriate values, and label it (P=).

Laura began the workday...

...by spending 15 minutes checking the bills for pricing errors, as well as quantity errors, address errors, and incomplete information. She also calculated the percentage of bills that were defective for 20 days. She then plotted the individual percentages, connected the line, and calculated the average percent defective, or P (see Diagram #10.2).

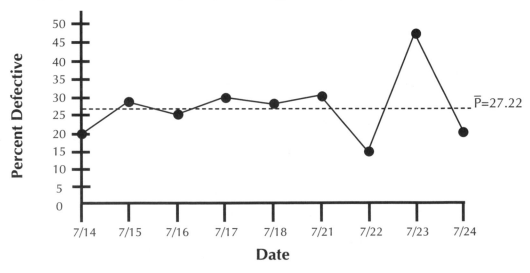

Diagram #10.2 — Plot the Data

Step 4:
Calculate the Control Limits

Control limits will tell you if your process is in statistical control (i.e., the process is exhibiting only common cause variation, or the usual amount of day-to-day variation you might expect from common reasons, such as slightly different materials, methods, machines, etc.). Think of control limits as invisible boundary lines. As long as the data points are within the boundary lines, everything is "OK." However, when data points are outside the boundary, alarms should go off, and you'll need to investigate why the boundary has been crossed. Control limits are calculated by using the following formula:

Upper Control Limit (UCL_p)	Lower Control Limit (LCL_p)
$UCL_p = \overline{P} + 3\sqrt{\dfrac{\overline{P} \times (100\% - \overline{P})}{n}}$	$LCL_p = \overline{P} - 3\sqrt{\dfrac{\overline{P} \times (100\% - \overline{P})}{n}}$
$= 27.22\% + 3\sqrt{\dfrac{27.22 \times (100\% - 27.22\%)}{50}}$	$= 27.22\% - 3\sqrt{\dfrac{27.22 \times (100\% - 27.22\%)}{50}}$
$= 27.22\% + 3\sqrt{\dfrac{27.22 \times 72.78\%}{50}}$	$= 27.22\% - 3\sqrt{\dfrac{27.22 \times 72.78\%}{50}}$
$= 27.22\% + 3\sqrt{39.62}$	$= 27.22\% - 3\sqrt{39.62}$
$= 27.22\% + 3 \times 6.29$	$= 27.22\% - 3 \times 6.29$
$= 46.10\%$	$= 8.35\%$

Where:
UCL_p = Upper Control Limit
LCL_p = Lower Control Limit
$\sqrt{}$ = Square Root
n = Sample Size
$\overline{P}$ = Average Percent Defective

Diagram #10.3 — Calculate Control Limits

Having plotted all the data points...

...Laura calculated the upper and lower control limits for the billing process (see Diagram #10.3). She found the corresponding points on the vertical axis of the graph and drew the horizontal lines above and below the average line. She labeled them with the upper and lower control limit values (see Diagram #10.4)...

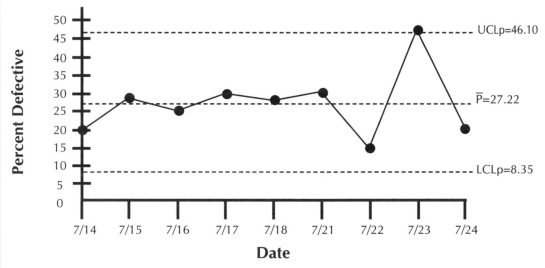

Diagram #10.4 — Plot Control Limits

Follow Up:
Agree on Next Steps

What you do next depends upon whether or not your points are within the control limits.

If all points are within the control limits:

- Continue with no changes.
- Recreate the P-Chart periodically to double-check process control.
- Make improvements to the process to reduce common variations.
- Review to ensure any changes have had a positive effect.

If one or more points are outside the control limits:

- Investigate and take steps to eliminate the cause(s).
- Review to ensure changes have had a positive effect (i.e., uncommon causes have been eliminated).
- Take new samples, and create a new P-Chart using limits based on the new information.

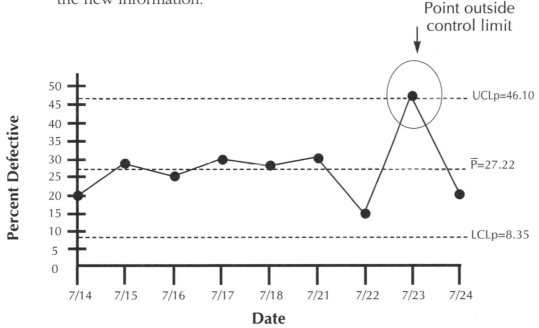

Diagram #10.5 — Identify Points Outside Control Limits

Having found the billing process to be out of control...

...(i.e., one or more points outside the control limits; see Diagram #10.5), Laura and two other billing analysts began an investigation into the causes. They knew that process improvements could not take place until all special causes, those which caused the data to be outside the control limits, had been identified and eliminated. From recent training they knew that special causes could be assigned to several main categories, including:

- Equipment or Materials
- Methods (i.e., not having a consistent method for the process)
- People (i.e., not having the necessary training, etc.)
- Environment (i.e., literally: a heat wave, earthquake, etc., or new management, company direction, etc.)

Summary

In summary, use the Control Chart when:

- Trying to determine if a process is in statistical control (i.e., a process is said to be "out of control" when a data point falls outside of the control limits).

- You want to create a visual representation of process performance. Like the Run Chart, the Control Chart provides a picture of process performance that can be used as a process tracking device.

- You want to distinguish between special cause variation (a clear occurrence of something not normally part of the process) and common cause variation (coincidental changes that are inherent in the process).

- You know the process will not change while you are collecting data. The process must not be changed because the intent is to see how the process performs "naturally."

Chapter Ten Review

List two uses for a Control Chart.

_____

_____

_____

_____

What does it mean for a process to be "out of control"?

_____

_____

_____

What steps could you take if your Control Chart shows one or more points outside the control limits?

_____

_____

_____

What specific opportunities do you have in your organization to use Control Charts?

_____

_____

_____

_____

What will you be measuring in these situations?

_____

_____

_____

NOTES

NOTES

NOTES

NOTES

NOTES